From Idea Into House

ROLF MYLLER, A.I.A.

House Designed by Myller & Szwarce
Drawings for this book prepared by Henry K. Szwarce

ATHENEUM 1974 NEW YORK

Library of Congress Cataloging in Publication Data

Myller, Rolf.

SUMMARY: Describes the process of building a house including
buying the land, drawing up plans, and the actual construction.
1. Architecture, Domestic — Designs and plans — Juvenile literature. 2. House construction — Juvenile literature. [1. Architecture, Domestic — Designs and plans. 2. House construction] I. Title.
NA7120.M95   728   73-84832
ISBN 0-689-30144-8

Library of Congress catalog card number 73-84832
ISBN 0-689-30144-8
Published simultaneously in Canada by McClelland & Stewart, Ltd.
Manufactured in the United States of America
Printed by Connecticut Printers, Inc., Hartford
Bound by A. Horowitz & Sons, New York
First Edition

To Elise, Corinne and Lois W. (S.) Myller

And to all the Ylvisakers
for whom the house was actually created

Metric Equivalents in Millimeters for Feet and Inches

Inches	Feet										
	0	1	2	3	4	5	6	7	8	9	10
0		305	610	914	1219	1524	1829	2134	2438	2743	3048
1/4	006	311	616	921	1225	1530	1835	2140	2445	2749	3054
1/2	013	317	622	927	1232	1537	1841	2146	2451	2756	3061
3/4	019	324	629	933	1238	1543	1848	2153	2457	2762	3067
1	025	330	635	940	1245	1549	1854	2159	2464	2769	3073
1/4	032	336	641	946	1251	1556	1860	2165	2470	2775	3080
1/2	038	343	648	952	1257	1562	1867	2172	2476	2781	3086
3/4	044	349	654	959	1264	1568	1873	2178	2483	2788	3092
2	051	356	660	965	1270	1575	1880	2184	2489	2794	3099
1/4	057	362	667	971	1276	1581	1886	2191	2495	2800	3105
1/2	063	368	673	978	1283	1587	1892	2197	2502	2807	3111
3/4	070	375	679	984	1289	1594	1899	2203	2508	2813	3118
3	076	381	686	991	1295	1600	1905	2210	2515	2819	3124
1/4	082	387	692	997	1302	1606	1911	2216	2521	2826	3130
1/2	089	394	698	1003	1308	1613	1918	2222	2527	2832	3137
3/4	095	400	705	1010	1314	1619	1924	2229	2534	2838	3143
4	102	406	711	1016	1321	1626	1930	2235	2540	2845	3149
1/4	108	413	717	1022	1327	1632	1937	2241	2546	2851	3156
1/2	114	419	724	1029	1333	1638	1943	2248	2553	2857	3162
3/4	121	425	730	1035	1340	1645	1949	2254	2559	2864	3168
5	127	432	737	1041	1346	1651	1956	2261	2565	2870	3175
1/4	133	438	743	1048	1352	1657	1962	2267	2572	2876	3181
1/2	140	444	750	1054	1359	1664	1968	2273	2578	2883	3188
3/4	146	451	756	1060	1365	1670	1975	2280	2584	2889	3194
6	152	457	762	1067	1372	1676	1981	2286	2591	2896	3200
1/4	159	463	768	1073	1378	1683	1987	2292	2597	2902	3207
1/2	165	470	775	1079	1384	1689	1994	2299	2603	2908	3213
3/4	171	476	781	1086	1391	1695	2000	2305	2610	2915	3219
7	178	483	787	1092	1397	1702	2007	2311	2616	2921	3226
1/4	184	489	794	1098	1403	1708	2013	2318	2622	2927	3232
1/2	190	495	800	1105	1410	1714	2019	2324	2629	2934	3238
3/4	197	502	806	1111	1416	1721	2026	2330	2636	2940	3245
8	203	508	813	1118	1422	1727	2032	2337	2642	2946	3251
1/4	209	514	819	1124	1429	1733	2038	2343	2648	2953	3257
1/2	216	521	825	1130	1435	1740	2045	2349	2654	2959	3264
3/4	222	527	832	1137	1441	1746	2051	2356	2661	2965	3270
9	229	533	838	1143	1448	1753	2057	2362	2667	2972	3276
1/4	235	540	844	1149	1454	1759	2064	2368	2673	2978	3283
1/2	241	546	851	1156	1460	1765	2070	2375	2680	2984	3289
3/4	248	552	857	1162	1467	1772	2076	2381	2686	2991	3295
10	254	559	864	1168	1473	1778	2083	2388	2692	2997	3302
1/4	260	565	870	1175	1479	1784	2089	2394	2699	3003	3308
1/2	267	571	876	1181	1486	1791	2095	2400	2705	3010	3315
3/4	273	578	883	1187	1492	1797	2102	2407	2711	3016	3321
11	279	584	889	1194	1499	1803	2108	2413	2718	3023	3327
1/4	286	590	895	1200	1505	1810	2114	2419	2724	3029	3334
1/2	292	597	902	1206	1511	1816	2121	2426	2730	3035	3340
3/4	298	603	908	1213	1518	1822	2127	2432	2737	3042	3346

At the time of this publication, it is expected that the Congress of the United States will pass legislation that will change the conventional measurement standard of feet and inches to the metric system.

Our customary measures in construction get complex and confusing. For example:

we call for an ordinary 2×4, but we really mean $1^5/_8''\times3^5/_8''$ piece of wood;

when the architect needs a $24'\,8^1/_2''$ dimension, the engineer marks the plot plan 24.70833.

when we discuss roofing material, we refer to "squares," which are areas of $10'\times10'$

on the same roof we use copper flashing, which is specified in terms of ounces; the metal thickness of doors is supplied in gauges.

it becomes a special problem when several dimensions like this, have to be added:

$4'\,7^5/_8''+17'\,0^7/_{32}''+1^1/_2''+12^7/_{16}''$ (it comes out to $22'\,9^{25}/_{32}''$)

there is also the thing that it takes eight $^1/_8''$ to make $1''$, 12 inches to make one foot, of which in turn three equal one yard.

Square yards are used to express measurements of drapery and carpet, and square feet are used for floor tiles. There are nine square feet in each square yard, and when we use earth to fill a hole we naturally have to use cubic yards. How many cubic feet are in every cubic yard?

and so on.

Even though this conventional system of measuring is currently in use, this book uses the metric system because it is much easier and makes more sense.

A meter is a little longer than three feet or one yard. Anyone capable of making change from a dollar can understand the meter, which is 100 centimeters or 1000 millimeters.

Introduction

When we look around us, it seems that there is always some type of construction going on; usually there is a big mess, lots of noise, and if we follow the progress of the activity long enough, we eventually see a building growing up from the ground.

What we are watching is actually only part of the story of how a building is born. All buildings start with an idea, which is based on a need for a building, whether the need is for a new house, a new school or even for a new forty-story office building.

Even though the buildings are different in size and appearance, the story of how such buildings are created usually follows the same pattern.

Once the right site is found to build on, after the need for the building has been established, an architect will design the building; his job is to organize the spaces, and after visualizing how the building will look and feel to be in, he prepares the drawings from which the builder can build the building.

In this book, a house has been used to illustrate this growing process because a house is the type of building most of us know best.

Most houses are built by a builder who uses one set of basic plans for many houses, and as a result all the houses look similar.

They are designed for what the builder considers the average family, and then each individual family must fit itself into the general plan. However, sometimes, a house is designed for just one specific family, and the result is a house that is special, and there is no other house like it.

When the architect makes a plan for such a house, the process he goes through is much the same, technically, whether the house is going to be repeated many times or is to be used only one time. The only difference is that when he is designing a house for one family, he must work closely with that family to know exactly what must go into that house.

To see how a house is made, let's take a look at what might happen to a family, whom we will call the Kummerfelds. Let's suppose that in this family there are a mother and father and two children, Tia and Tom.

Chapter One

If the Kummerfeld family agreed on anything, it was that they needed a house. The apartment they lived in was far too small. There was only one bathroom, and everyone wanted to be in it at the same time in the morning. Tia Kummerfeld needed a bigger closet and more space for her books, and Tom's rock collection was spilling all over the hall. Mother said the kitchen had no room for anything. And Dad wanted a place where he could have some peace and quiet.

But no matter where the Kummerfelds went or how hard they looked, they couldn't seem to find what they wanted. Every weekend they drove around in search of houses for sale. They looked at big houses, and they looked at small ones; they saw new houses, and they saw old ones. But each one they saw was either too large or too small, too expensive, or had something about it that they didn't like. There were even houses that looked just right, but somehow just didn't feel like home to the Kummerfelds.

"I wish we could find a house just like my friend George has. He's got plenty of room, and he doesn't have his old sister always breathing down his neck, either," Tom said.

"George's home is nice," said Dad. "And your sister needs more room as much as you do."

One spring day, on the way to look at one more house, they passed a field full of blooming daisies.

"Let's pick some, please," begged Tia.

"They'll die before we get home," grumbled Tom.

However, Mr. Kummerfeld stopped the car on the side of the road, and they all got out.

Tia ran to the meadow, and Tom headed for an old gnarled apple tree near the middle of the field.

Dad followed with his arm around Mom's shoulder. They stopped and admired the view into the valley that stretched out beyond.

"What a place for someone's living room," said Mrs. Kummerfeld.

"Isn't it though," Dad agreed, and then after pausing he said, "Hey, why not ours?"

Tia came running up with her bouquet of daisies, holding them out to be admired.

finding land

"I was just saying," her father told her, "that it would be great if we could build our house right here. What do you think, pussycat?"

Tia let out a whoop. "I want my room to have a big window right here," she chirped, "so I can see the daisies all the time!" She pointed to a place where the daisies were growing in great, dense bunches.

"Not all the time, dear," said Mom. "Remember that there's snow on the ground in winter. And besides, we don't even know if this land is for sale."

"Or if we could afford it," added Dad. "But it is something to think about."

They looked at each other for a moment, and then the three of them grinned in agreement.

"Look at me," Tom yelled, to get their attention. He was high in the apple tree, where he had found a perfect sitting place.

"Come on down, you ape," Tia yelled. "We're going to buy this land and build a house."

The three turned back toward the car as Tom slid down the tree and came running up.

"What did you say?" he asked.

They told him, and by the time they reached the car, Tom was putting the finishing touches on a perfect tree house, while the others were all talking about what they wanted. Dad would have a private study. And Mom wanted a window at the front of the house so she could see who was coming down the road.

"You mean the back of the house, don't you," Tia corrected her.

"Either," said Dad. "Our house is going to look so great from all sides that it won't really have a back or a front. The front of the house will be wherever you are."

"Can't you see it there in the middle of the field with its white walls, sitting among the daisies?..." Mom said.

"I thought it was going to have wood shingles," said Dad, laughing. "But let's argue about that when the time comes. Meanwhile, I know just the spot for my vegetable garden."

"You won't let them cut down my tree, will you, Dad?" asked Tom.

"Of course not," said Dad. "But let's be realistic. We don't even know if the land is for sale. And even if it is, it's probably too expensive. And even if we should be able to afford it, the location may not be right. Is there a decent school nearby, are there stores, is there a train station so I can get to work?"

They rode along in silence, each thinking his own thoughts, until they came to some buildings.

"Look," said Mom, "there's a real estate office. Let's at least ask about the land. Nothing ventured, nothing gained."

Dad stopped, but he warned, "Don't get your hopes up too much. This realtor may not even know about the land."

"Why stop here?" asked Tom. "Why can't you just find the owner and buy it?"

the realtor "A realtor helps you find the owner if you want to buy land, or he helps find a buyer if you want to sell it." Dad explained. "The person who sells the land pays the real estate dealer a commission on the amount he receives."

"Why is it all so complicated?" Tom asked.

Dad laughed and shook his head.

The family went into the office, where the realtor turned out to be a very attractive woman. She asked how she could be of help.

All four Kummerfelds started to talk at once. And the woman

laughed and held up her hand. "One at a time," she said.

So Dad explained about the land they had seen.

"It is for sale," she said. "I had a call just the other day from the owner. He's been holding on to it, hoping to build on it himself. But he's about to be transferred by his company so he has to sell. It's a great piece of land. I've been out there, though I haven't had time to get a sign on it yet. There's a school near enough to walk, and there's a shopping center at the crossroads about a half-mile away. The train is nearby, only about ten minutes by car."

"Enough!" said Mr. Kummerfeld. "We're sold. But I'm not sure I can afford it. How much does he want?"

The woman named a price, and Dad frowned.

"A little more than I had hoped to pay," he said. "But what about taxes in this area? How is the land zoned? Are there going to be any more shopping centers around? It's nice to have one near, but we don't want one across the street. And are there electricity, water and sewers?"

The woman nodded and began to answer his questions. Then Mom asked more questions, but Tia and Tom grew restless and gave up listening after a while.

In her mind, Tia was back in the daisy field and Tom was climbing the apple tree, building his tree house, when Dad said to them, "Well, how about it? Still want that lot?"

"Yes!" they both shouted. "Oh, yes. Can we afford to buy it?"

Dad grinned. "Well, I guess we can, but it is more than I think I ought to pay." He turned again to the realtor. "Do you think the owner will come down?"

"I can call him right now," she said. "He's anxious to sell, so I think he will." She disappeared into another room, and in a few minutes she was back. "He'll consider it," she said. "I think that means he'll do it."

a binder "Do you want a binder?" Mr. Kummerfeld asked.

"Yes, if you please," the woman answered. "A small amount will do."

"Do you mean you have to pay when you're not even sure you can buy it?" Tom asked.

"Just enough to show that I really want the land," Dad answered. "It keeps anyone else from buying it for the next few days, while we see if we can work out a deal."

He wrote his check, and then everyone shook hands all around.

Out of the office, Mom gave Dad a big hug. Tom picked up a rock and threw it at a tree, which he decided wasn't half as nice as his apple tree. And Tia thought again about the daisies and the room that was going to be big enough for all her books and other things. Maybe even big enough to have a girl friend overnight sometimes.

the title search

The next day Dad went to see a lawyer. Tia wondered why that was necessary, and Dad explained that he didn't know all the legal things he needed to know to be sure everything was all right in the contract he would sign for the land. Also, the lawyer would check the old records and deeds at City Hall to make sure the owner really did own it. Not that the owner would try to cheat them on purpose. But it could happen, for instance, that the owner's grandfather had given him the land and then some other time, forgetting the first gift, had given all or part of the land to someone else. "It's happened," Dad said. "And we don't want to build our house on land that turns out not to be ours."

Several days went by. "Is the land ours yet?" Tia asked every day.

"Not yet," her father said. "Just be patient. It takes time. In fact, it will probably take a couple of weeks, maybe even a month before all of the papers are signed."

"I didn't think it would take so long," Tia complained.

"Wait until we start building a house," Dad said, teasing her. "Then you'll really be impatient."

Finally the title search was over. The owner did really own the land; he had title to the property. And he and Dad had agreed on a price. So one day the owner, his lawyer, the real estate dealer, and all of the Kummerfelds and their lawyer met in the lawyer's office. This meeting was the closing—the time when the deal would be closed. All the problems that had not been settled before, were settled at the meeting, and everyone made sure he understood all that was going to be agreed to.

"I didn't know there was an easement on the property," Mr. Kummerfeld said at one point. Tia opened her ears. Easement sounded dangerous.

"The electric company has the right to go over or under a part of your land," said the owner's lawyer. "But the place they want is far enough from where you want to build your house that it shouldn't be any bother."

Dad nodded, and the talk went on. After the owner had agreed to share the cost of the taxes for that year with Mr. Kummerfeld, a contract

the closing   was signed by both of them. The contract stated in writing exactly what they had agreed on, so that there would be no misunderstanding in the future. Each of them received a copy of the contract for their records.

The whole family was at the table as Mr. Kummerfeld signed a check and gave it to the owner in payment for the land. The owner gave the realtor a check, which was her commission for finding the buyer, and then turned to Mr. Kummerfeld and handed him the deed. It gave the title of the property to Mr. and Mrs. Kummerfeld, making them the legal owners of the land, complete with apple tree and daisies.

"Now are we really the owners of our land?" Tia asked as they left the office.

"We are," said Dad.

"Then how do we get our house on it?"

"Good question," said Dad. "I've already thought about it, and the other day when it looked as if the deal would go through today, I called the man who designed George's house, the one Tom likes so much. He's coming over for dinner tonight so we can talk about our house with him."

the architect   That night a young man wearing a rumply suit came in when Dad answered the door. Tia thought he didn't look too impressive. She wasn't sure he could really build a house.

"Are you the man who builds houses?" she asked.

"Not the man who builds them," he said, "but the man who designs them. I plan how the house will look and what will be in it. Then I get other people to build the house. I'm an architect."

Tia didn't know what to say, so she didn't say anything.

"Where's Tom?" Mom asked.

"In his room with his rock collection," Tia said. She ran to get him.

"The architect is here," she said. "But he doesn't build houses, he just plans them. I don't think we're ever going to get a house."

"We better get one soon," said Tom darkly, "or one of us has to move out."

"You, you oaf!" Tia said.

"What's the problem?" asked Dad.

"Tom says that if we don't have a new house soon, one of us has to move out of here. There isn't room for all of us anymore. And I said that if anyone is going to move out, it has to be he."

The architect laughed. "We'd better get started on your house plans right away. I'd hate to see the family break up just because you didn't get a new house in time."

"We have time enough to eat first," said Mrs. Kummerfeld, with a frown at Tia and Tom. "Then we can talk about our house."

But before they were through eating, they were all talking about what they wanted in the house. The architect listened carefully and in turn asked questions. Who did the cooking in the family and where did they like to eat best? What kind of parties did they have and how many people did they invite? Who in the family liked to take baths and who preferred showers?

"Why do you need to know all that?" Tom asked.

"So the house will fit all the things you do," said the architect. "And now I'd like to see what you have here."

He looked at every room very carefully and took notes about all the furniture. Mom suggested in each room that they needed more storage space. "There can never be too much," she said.

Tia showed the architect her books and suggested that she'd like a room big enough so a friend could spend the night.

Tom pointed out his rock collection spread all over the floor, and his insect collection, which he kept on a shelf in the closet.

"Can you please provide a special place for them?" Mom pleaded. "I really expect those cockroaches to come alive every time I open that closet."

The architect gave Tom a wink and assured Mom that he would try to remember.

After the architect's visit, nothing seemed to happen. The family went out and had a picnic on their land one Sunday. It was just as nice as they remembered, even nicer, because now it belonged to them. But it would be better when they could stay there all the time.

"How soon will it be?" Tia asked.

"Not very soon, I'm afraid," said Dad. "Tom is just going to have to hold his collections down. And you're going to have to get all of your books from the library for a while."

It seemed ages, but it was only a couple of weeks later when they met at the architect's office. It was a bright and pleasant place. The walls were decorated with photographs of the buildings he had designed and drawings of houses that hadn't been built yet.

"Which one of these will our house look like?" Tom asked.

"Not any of them," said the architect. "Your house will be made to fit your family, not to look like someone else's house."

He introduced them to his assistants, the draftsmen, who were drawing at large drafting boards.

Then the Kummerfelds and the architect met around a conference table, and the architect unrolled a drawing.

a survey   "This is a survey of your property," he explained. "It was made by my surveyor. He measured everything on the property. You can see the road and the apple tree. The broken lines around the edges are the boundary lines. You can't see them, of course, when you go out to look at the land, but it is important to know just where your land ends. The curving lines are the contours; they show how the land slopes."

Tia looked at the drawings and remembered the land as she had seen it. Soon it was clear to her where everything was. She pointed to the spot she had picked for her room. "I want to look out at the daisies," she said. "My window is here."

"This is where the kitchen ought to be," said Mrs. Kummerfeld. "Then I'll be able to see the road."

"This level land, here, will be the right place for a vegetable garden," said Dad.

Tom did not say anything. But he studied each line, as if he were trying to imagine just where the house would be and what it would look like.

Finally the architect picked up a roll of tracing paper and took a soft black pencil. He laid the paper over the survey and explained that he was going to make a flow diagram. This was an abstract sketch that explored how the house could fit on the land, how different areas related, and how it all should work to fit the family. He started doodling and while he was doodling, he mumbled. It wasn't clear whether he was talking to himself or to the Kummerfelds.

"Let's not get hung up on the details, but keeping them in mind, let's think about the things that matter most: the view (and he drew some arrows), the slope (and he drew some curves), and how we move around (and he drew some squiggles). But first let's see how we get in and out (and he drew some lines). This end can be the quiet area and this is where the action is. And here is a good place from which to see the daisies. How will it feel, what is the mood? It all has to work together, and this sure doesn't." He ended by crumpling up the sketches he had made and starting over on fresh paper. He mumbled some more; made some more strange marks. And after five or six attempts said, "I think I've got it."

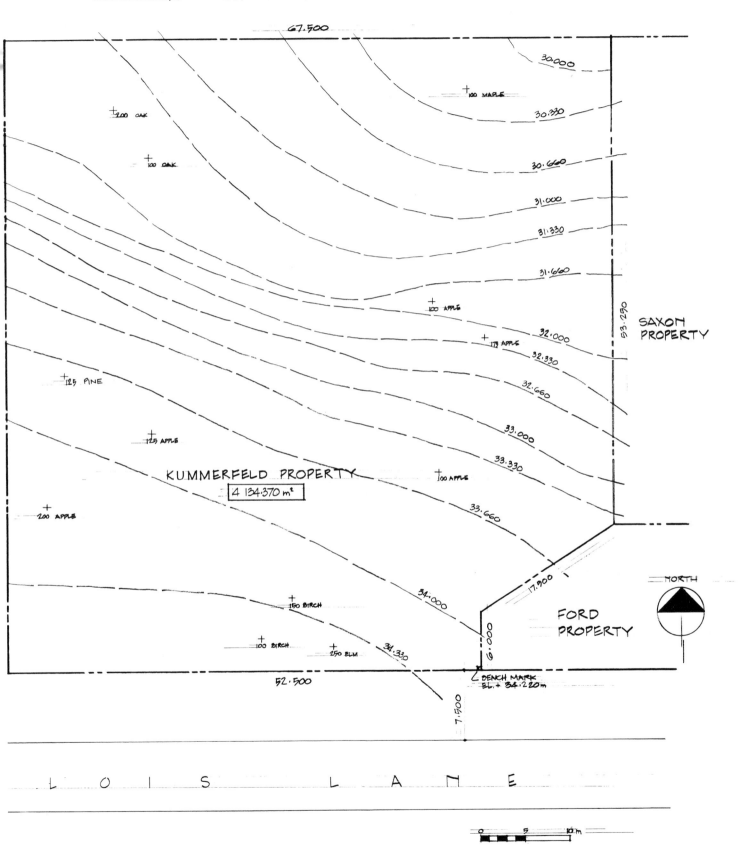

VILLAGE NATURE PRESERVE

67.500

30.000

+ 100 MAPLE

30.330

+ 200 OAK

+ 100 OAK

30.660

31.000

31.330

31.660

+ 100 APPLE

32.000

+ 175 APPLE

32.330

+ 125 PINE

32.660

+ 125 APPLE

33.000

33.330

KUMMERFELD PROPERTY

+ 100 APPLE

4 134.370 m²

33.660

+ 200 APPLE

53.290

SAXON
PROPERTY

34.000

17.900

NORTH

FORD
PROPERTY

+ 150 BIRCH

+ 100 BIRCH

+ 250 ELM

34.330

0.000

52.500

BENCH MARK
EL. + 34.220 m

7.500

L O I S   L A N E

0   5   10 m

a flow diagram

"Now if we come in here," he explained, "we get a feeling of the entire space—we will know, or better, we will feel the entire house. The entry hall has to be right near the kitchen, which should be near the dining area for easy serving. Since you don't want a formal dining room, let's use this space to eat in. How about that? You said that you don't entertain too often, and by creating a large area in the entry, we can get a space for eating, but use the entire space as a visual experience that can be appreciated all the time and not only during meals. Hey, let's put an interior garden right in here, too, to protect the dining area from the entry space. You can have a garden that works summer or winter. And here is the area for the adults and here is the area for children, close to each other, yet completely separate." He went on and on until he had determined the general location of everything they had discussed, right down to Dad's vegetable garden.

The Kummerfelds looked on, fascinated. The architect had drawn a series of shapes and lines, all in a very rough form.

"But that doesn't look like a real house," said Tia. "It only seems like a house when you talk about it. It sounds more like a house than it looks like one."

"Can I make a suggestion?" asked Tom.

"Of course," said the architect.

Tom took the black pencil. "The TV viewing area should be here," he said. "It's convenient for everyone, and the noise won't bother Mom and Dad."

Everyone looked at Tom in surprise.

"I should have thought of that myself," said the architect. "You're exactly right."

"But when does it begin to look like a house?" Tia asked.

"Next time you see me, we'll have something that looks more like a house," the architect assured her.

"We need this house soon," Tom said.

"I know, or someone has to move out of your apartment before the house is built," said the architect. "Well, I'll do my best."

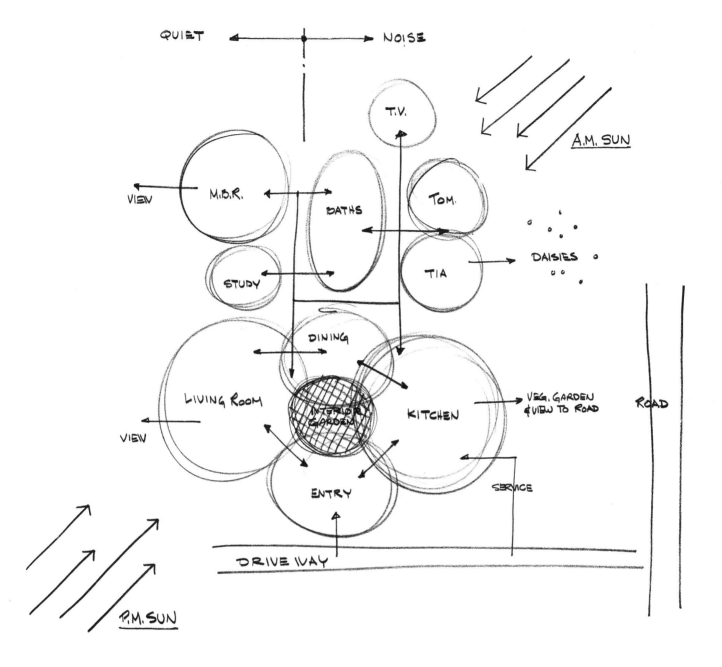

Another long time went by. It began to seem as if they would never have a house. Tia almost forgot sometimes that they were going to move out of their old cramped quarters. And sometimes she agreed with Tom that someone was going to have to leave the apartment if something didn't happen soon.

the plans   At last the architect called and said he had something for them to see. When they arrived at his office, he led them to the conference table again. This time there were no survey drawings; instead there was a group of drawings each marked,

RESIDENCE OF MR. AND MRS. RONALD KUMMERFIELD

"This is a floor plan," the architect said to Tia and Tom. "It's as if you had cut the roof off the house and were looking down on the rooms from above. You can tell how thick the walls are; you can see each room and how it's furnished. The doors are where there is a piece of wall missing, and the windows are these thin lines in the outside walls."

"Yes, I know all that," said Tia impatiently, because it was very clear.

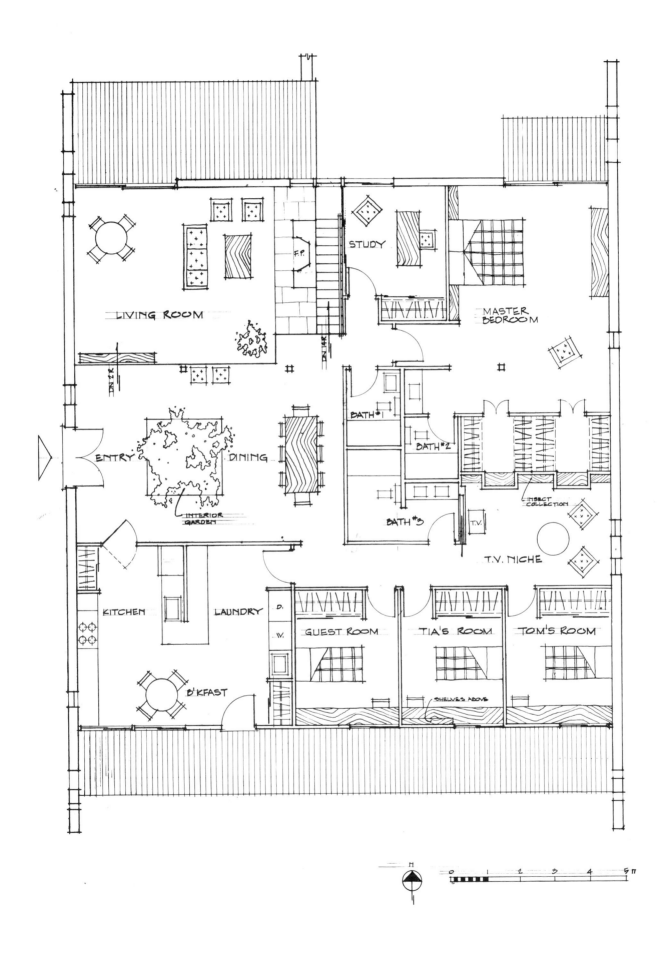

LIVING ROOM

F.P.

STUDY

MASTER
BEDROOM

DN 14 R

DN 2 R

ENTRY

DINING

INTERIOR
GARDEN

BATH #1

BATH #2

BATH #3

T.V.

INSECT
COLLECTION

T.V. NICHE

KITCHEN

LAUNDRY

D.

W.

GUEST ROOM

TIA'S ROOM

TOM'S ROOM

B'KFAST

SHELVES ABOVE

N

0   1   2   3   4   5 M

And the only thing that really interested her was the space marked TIA'S ROOM. There was room enough, she could see, for her bed and dresser. The closet was large, and there were going to be bookcases on one wall. She was delighted to discover a large window from which she was sure she could see the meadow with the daisies. But the furniture drawn in helped to give her a feeling of the size of the room.

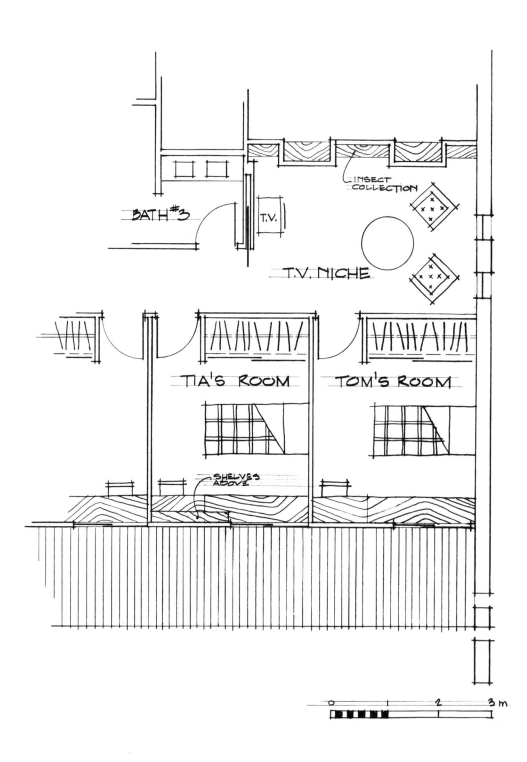

BATH #3

T.V.

INSECT COLLECTION

T.V. NICHE

TIA'S ROOM

TOM'S ROOM

SHELVES ABOVE

0   1   2   3 m

Tom studied the part of the plan marked TOM'S ROOM first. All his furniture was there. And there were shelves marked Insect Collection and Rock Collection.

"What's this," he asked, pointing to the closet. "What does that dotted line mean?"

"A shelf in the closet," said the architect. "Anything that happens above floor level is usually shown in dotted lines."

Outside the space for the rooms marked TOM'S ROOM and TIA'S ROOM, Tom now saw a space marked TV.

"Gee," he said in surprise, looking up at the architect, "you really did it. You made the TV room where I said."

"Of course," said the architect, laughing. "I told you it was a good idea. And I gave you plenty of room for lounging around, and for friends to watch, too."

Meanwhile Mom and Dad had been looking over the rest of the house.

"It's all here," said Dad, looking up pleased. "How did you manage to take in so much of our furniture in one visit?"

"It's my job," said the architect with false modesty.

"And everything else is here, too," said Mom. "The living room looks over the valley. The kitchen faces the road, and it has plenty of storage space. Just look at all the closets! It will be a blessing to have more than one bathroom, too. And I think I'm going to love that inside garden. Have you ever done that before?"

"No," said the architect, pleased. "But I like the idea. I think it's an ideal way to separate the hall and the dining area. Now I want you to take a look at the outside of the house." He held up a large drawing.

"We can't take a photograph of it, of course, because it doesn't exist yet. But this is the next best thing—a perspective drawing, which gives a realistic three-dimensional impression."

He went on speaking before anyone had a chance to comment on the picture.

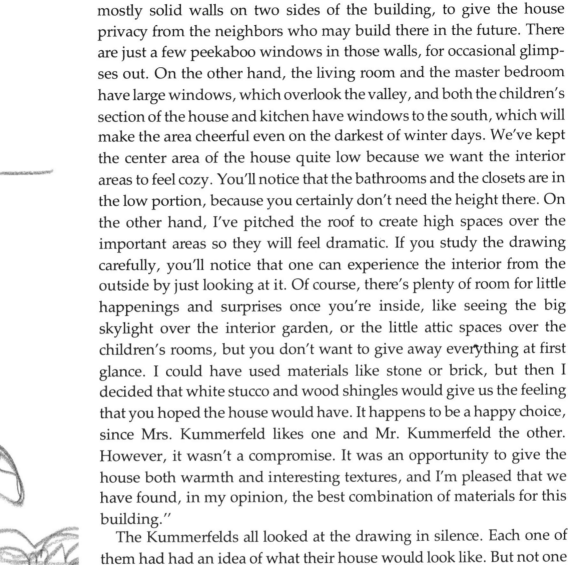

"The appearance of the exterior of the house is really the natural outgrowth of what happens inside. You will notice I've designed mostly solid walls on two sides of the building, to give the house privacy from the neighbors who may build there in the future. There are just a few peekaboo windows in those walls, for occasional glimpses out. On the other hand, the living room and the master bedroom have large windows, which overlook the valley, and both the children's section of the house and kitchen have windows to the south, which will make the area cheerful even on the darkest of winter days. We've kept the center area of the house quite low because we want the interior areas to feel cozy. You'll notice that the bathrooms and the closets are in the low portion, because you certainly don't need the height there. On the other hand, I've pitched the roof to create high spaces over the important areas so they will feel dramatic. If you study the drawing carefully, you'll notice that one can experience the interior from the outside by just looking at it. Of course, there's plenty of room for little happenings and surprises once you're inside, like seeing the big skylight over the interior garden, or the little attic spaces over the children's rooms, but you don't want to give away everything at first glance. I could have used materials like stone or brick, but then I decided that white stucco and wood shingles would give us the feeling that you hoped the house would have. It happens to be a happy choice, since Mrs. Kummerfeld likes one and Mr. Kummerfeld the other. However, it wasn't a compromise. It was an opportunity to give the house both warmth and interesting textures, and I'm pleased that we have found, in my opinion, the best combination of materials for this building."

The Kummerfelds all looked at the drawing in silence. Each one of them had had an idea of what their house would look like. But not one of them had thought of a house that looked like this. Yet as they looked, each of them realized that it did fit into his idea of what a nice house might look like. It was simple. It was beautiful. And it worked. It fit their needs. It really was a house made just for them.

"I like it," said Dad happily.

"So do I," said Mom.

"How soon will it be built?" asked Tia.

"Well, not by next week," said the architect. "I'm glad you like what you see. Now I can go to work on the final plans."

"More plans," said Tom, "What's wrong with these?"

"They're fine as far as they go," said the architect. "But the builder has to know just exactly what to use everywhere, down almost to the last nail and bolt. Those are the plans my draftsmen and I have to make now."

"Maybe we should leave and let him get to work," said Mr. Kummerfeld.

"We'll get started as soon as we can," said the architect. "And I'll be calling from time to time to check things out with you. It won't be long before your house will be on its way."

Chapter Two

working drawings

In the next few weeks the architect prepared the working drawings. These are drawings, as the name implies, that explain how the building works and how all the parts fit together.

There are so many things that happen at any one place in a building, that the architect needs several drawings of the same area to show what the carpenter needs to know, what the electrician has to put in, what the plumber has to do, and so on. If the architect were to include all the information on one drawing, there would be so many lines and notes on it that it would become confusing and hard to understand.

All the drawings work together, and there is no beginning, middle or end to them; one has to have them all to understand how the house should be built.

Some drawings are of the entire house showing the relationship of all the areas. Other drawings show parts of the house enlarged, so that the builder can see in detail exactly how to put them together.

The architect reviewed each drawing with the Kummerfelds and explained what each one represented.

the plot plan

The first drawing was the PLOT PLAN, which showed the builder exactly where the house would be located in relationship to the property lines. The drawing also indicated everything that happened on the property, outside of the actual building, such as the driveway, the paths, the important trees, and special landscape features like terracing and planting.

The curving lines on the drawing were the contours, which showed how the land sloped. The numbers on the contours indicated the vertical distance of every point along that line, in relation to a common spot defined as zero. Zero is the constant level of water in the ocean, measured at mean tide, the time when the water is exactly between high and low tide.

Where the contours were shown with broken lines, they were existing contours, and where the lines became solid, the builder was going to have to raise or lower the grade, or surface, of the land to the height or elevation marked.

By doing this, the architect was actually shaping the land as he pleased; and by controlling the slope of the land, he was allowing rain water to flow away from the building rather than toward it, to avoid problems like leaky basements.

Many special words were used on the drawings. These are explained in the glossary in the back of the book.

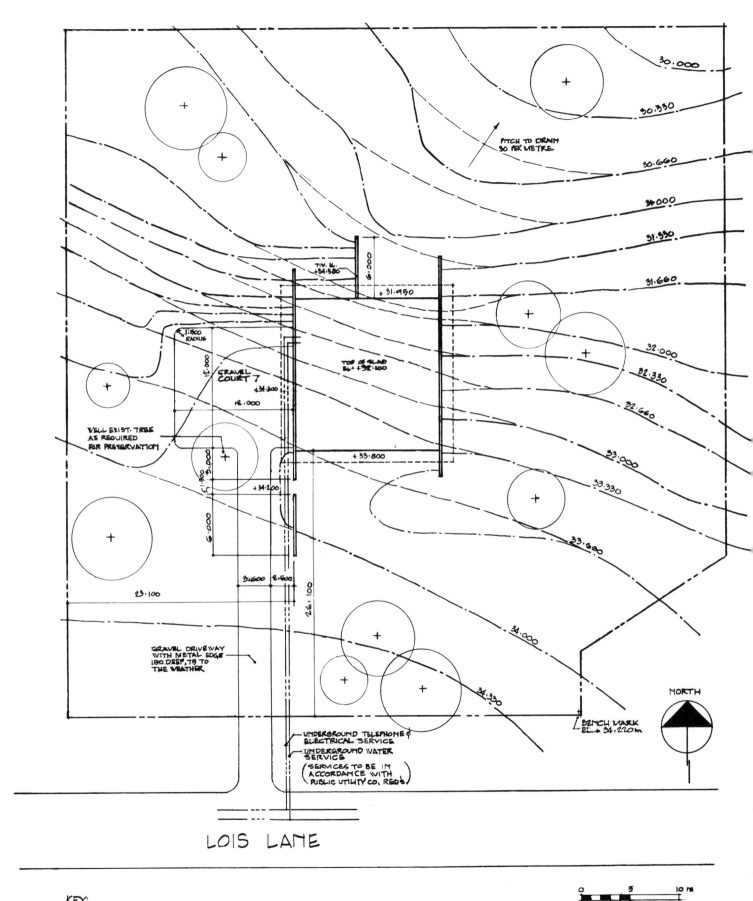

PITCH TO DRAIN
30 PER METRE

30.000
30.330
30.660
31.000
31.330
31.660
32.000
32.330
32.660
33.000
33.330
33.660
34.000
34.330

T.W. EL.
+34.550

6.000

+31.950

1.500
RADIUS

TOP OF SLAB
EL. +32.500

GRAVEL
COURT 7
+34.300

12.000

12.000

WELL EXIST. TREE
AS REQUIRED
FOR PRESERVATION

24.000

+33.800

21.500

+34.200

6.000

3.600 8.500

23.100

26.100

GRAVEL DRIVEWAY
WITH METAL EDGE
150 DEEP, 75 TO
THE WEATHER

NORTH

BENCH MARK
EL. + 34.220m

UNDERGROUND TELEPHONE &
ELECTRICAL SERVICE
UNDERGROUND WATER
SERVICE
(SERVICES TO BE IN
ACCORDANCE WITH
PUBLIC UTILITY CO. REQ'S.)

LOIS LANE

0   5   10 m

floor plans   The next drawings on the working drawings were the FLOOR PLANS, which explained the location of walls, openings, corners, and gave the sizes of all the rooms. The numbers between the dots (sometimes shown as arrows) spelled out the exact measurement or dimension between them. Since the FLOOR PLAN drawing was relatively small, certain areas were shown enlarged on other pages, allowing the architect to describe what was happening in greater detail.

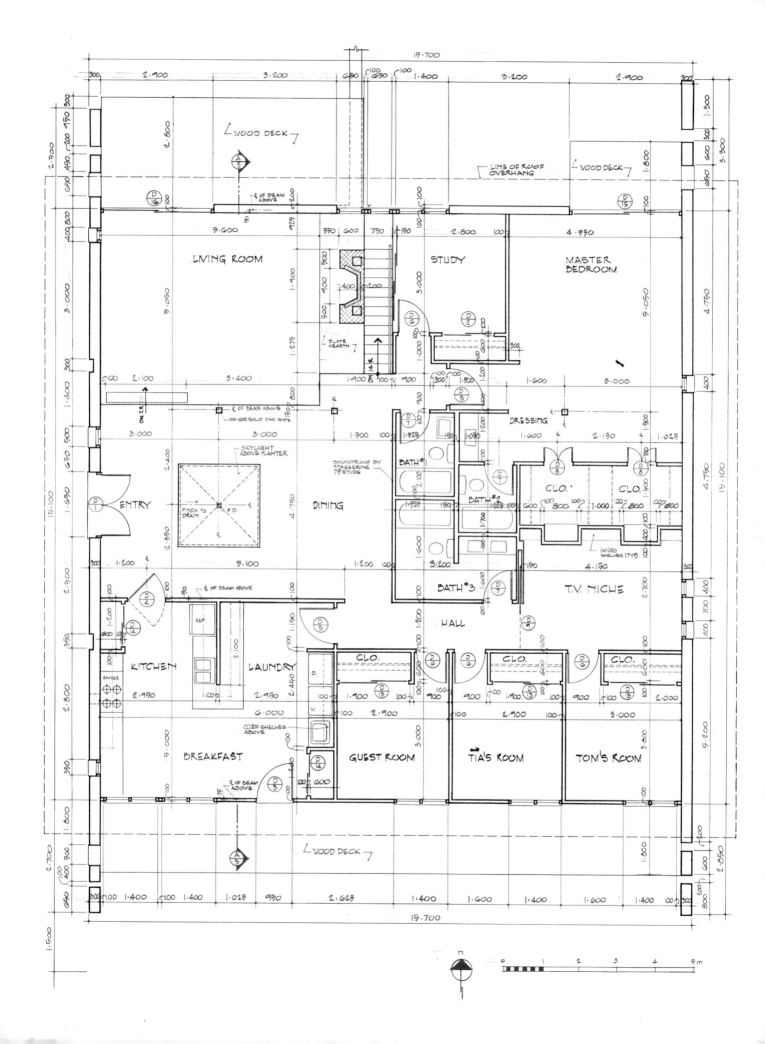

basement floor plans

The basement floor plan showed what happened directly below the first floor plan.

The drawings were very exact, because it would be embarrassing to the architect if the stairs on one plan were in a slightly different place on the other.

There were no garage plans in the working plans. The architect had eliminated the garage from the plans because Mr. Kummerfeld agreed that he would add it as a separate building in the future because he was afraid that the cost of the house would be too high.

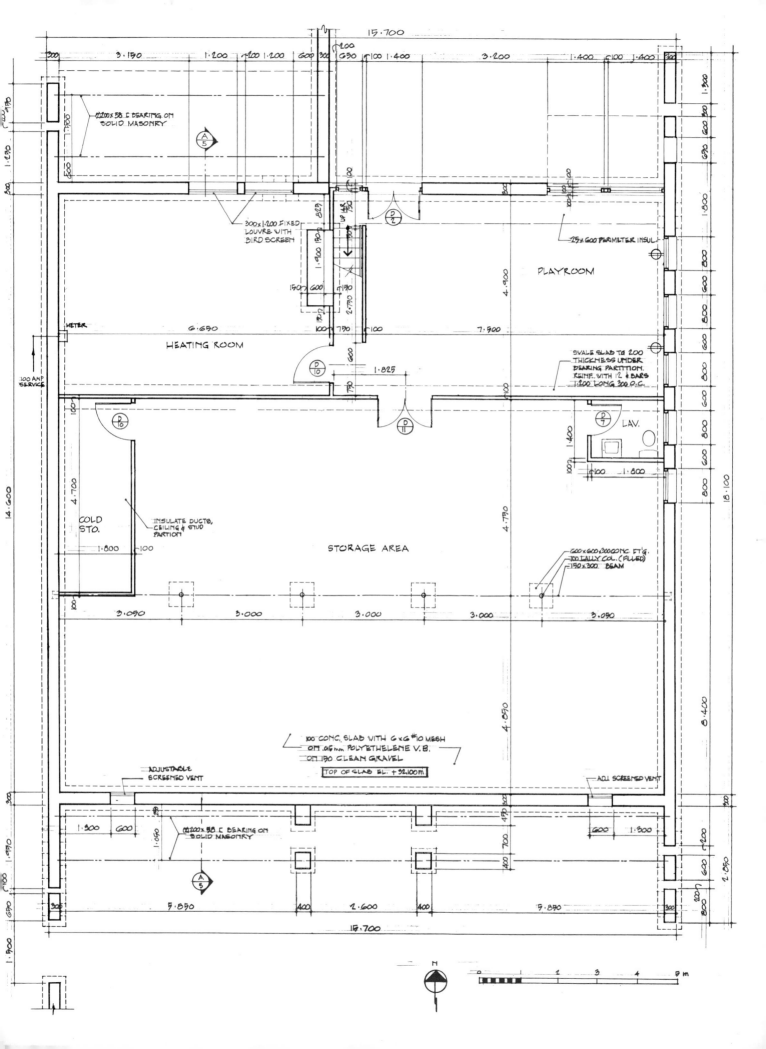

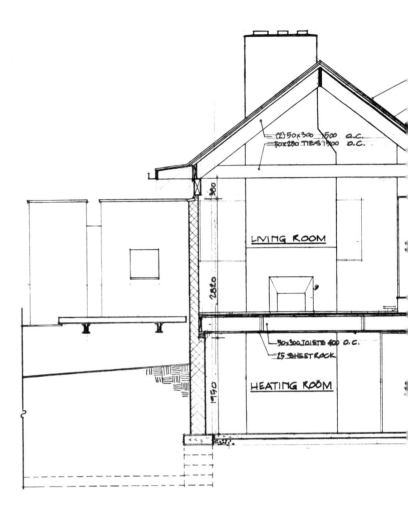

elevation

The large arrows marked _A_ were used to show where a cross section had been cut through the building. Sections were used to show what was inside and couldn't be seen by looking at the plan. It was, Tom thought, like looking at a layer cake. You cut the cake, in order to see what was inside, and this was like taking a section. A section of cake showed how many layers there were, whether they were chocolate or vanilla, and also just how thick the icing was, on both the top and around the edges.

Similarly, the section through the building showed clearly how high the ceilings were to be from the floor, what was in the walls and what was over and below them.

34

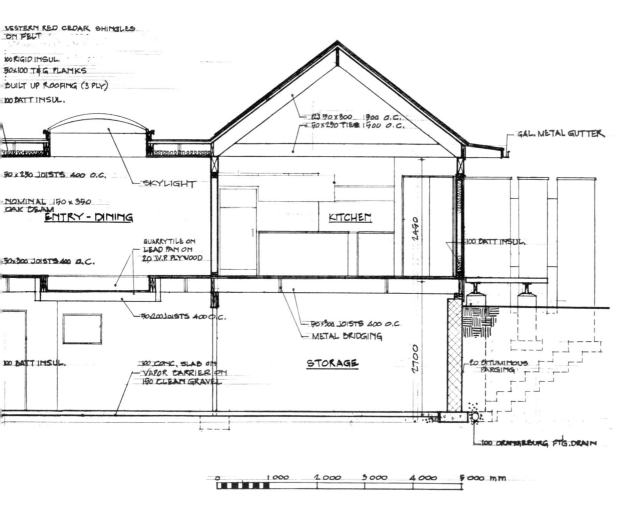

WESTERN RED CEDAR SHINGLES
ON FELT

100 RIGID INSUL.
50×100 T&G PLANKS
BUILT UP ROOFING (3 PLY)
100 BATT INSUL.

12 90×300   900 O.C.
50×250 TIES 1500 O.C.

GAL. METAL GUTTER

50×250 JOISTS 400 O.C.

SKYLIGHT

NOMINAL 150×350
OAK BEAM

ENTRY - DINING

KITCHEN

2450

100 BATT INSUL.

QUARRYTILE ON
LEAD PAN ON
20 W.P. PLYWOOD

50×300 JOISTS 400 O.C.

50×200 JOISTS 400 O.C.

50×300 JOISTS 400 O.C.
METAL BRIDGING

STORAGE

2700

100 BATT INSUL.

100 CONC. SLAB ON
VAPOR BARRIER ON
150 CLEAN GRAVEL

20 BITUMINOUS
PARGING

100 ORANGEBURG FTG. DRAIN

0   1000   2000   3000   4000   5000 mm

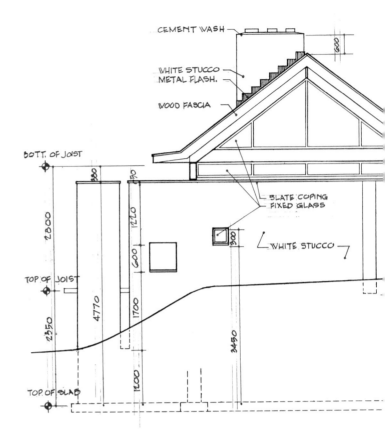

CEMENT WASH
WHITE STUCCO
METAL FLASH.
WOOD FASCIA

BOTT. OF JOIST

SLATE COPING
FIXED GLASS

WHITE STUCCO

TOP OF JOIST

TOP OF SLAB

elevation

The architect called the side views of the building elevations. These were drawings of the sides of the house, as they might be seen from the outside. On these the architect showed all the things that could not be described on the FLOOR PLANS. Here, for instance, was information about the height of the windows and exterior doors, the slope of the roofs and how far they would overhang, and how high the chimney would extend above the roof. Elevations also described the materials to be used on the outside, and showed how the house would look when it all was put together.

On the Kummerfelds' house, the side walls were extended beyond the building itself to give the Kummerfelds additional privacy from their neighbors. The architect left spaces and holes in the walls to avoid the cramped feeling the family might experience if the walls were left solid. He did it because it looked and felt better that way.

36

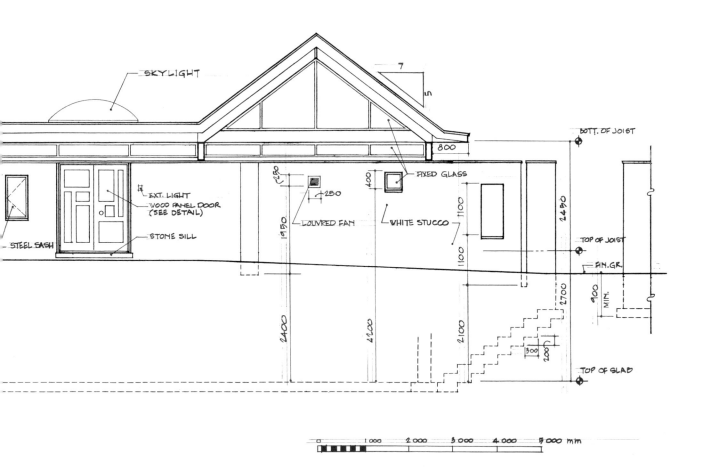

SKYLIGHT

7
5

BOTT. OF JOIST

800

FIXED GLASS

EXT. LIGHT
WOOD PANEL DOOR
(SEE DETAIL)

250
1950
400

250

LOUVRED FAN
WHITE STUCCO
STONE SILL

2490
1100
1100

STEEL SASH

TOP OF JOIST

FIN. GR.

900
MIN.

2400
4200
2100
2700

300
200

TOP OF SLAB

0   1 000   2 000   3 000   4 000   5 000 mm

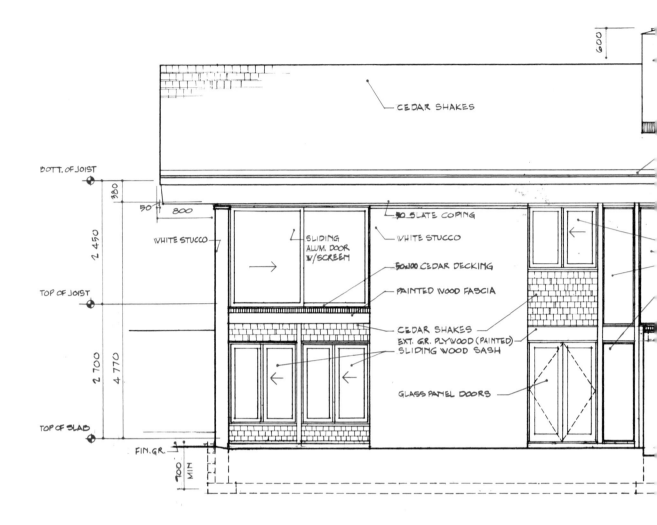

CEDAR SHAKES

BOTT. OF JOIST

380

50

800

WHITE STUCCO

2 450

TOP OF JOIST

2 700

4 770

TOP OF SLAB

FIN. GR.

700 MIN

600

50 SLATE COPING

WHITE STUCCO

SLIDING ALUM. DOOR W/SCREEN

50x100 CEDAR DECKING

PAINTED WOOD FASCIA

CEDAR SHAKES

EXT. GR. PLYWOOD (PAINTED)

SLIDING WOOD SASH

GLASS PANEL DOORS

elevation

38

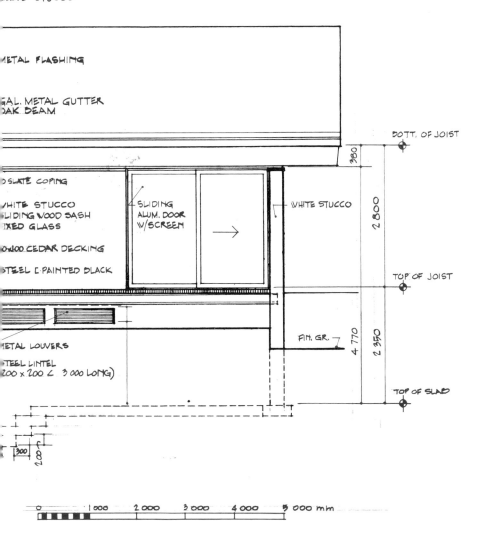

CEMENT WASH
WHITE STUCCO

METAL FLASHING

GAL. METAL GUTTER
OAK BEAM

BOTT. OF JOIST

380

SLATE COPING

WHITE STUCCO
SLIDING WOOD SASH
FIXED GLASS

SLIDING
ALUM. DOOR
W/SCREEN

WHITE STUCCO

2800

50x100 CEDAR DECKING

STEEL C-PAINTED BLACK

TOP OF JOIST

METAL LOUVERS

STEEL LINTEL
(200 x 200 L 3000 LONG)

FIN. GR.

4770

2350

TOP OF SLAB

300

200

0   1000   2000   3000   4000   5000 mm

Whenever something important was happening behind something else, it was indicated in dotted lines. It was a very convenient way of making it possible to look through something solid.

Remember the contour lines? Well, the architect had looked at the distance between them on the PLOT PLAN, and marked their relative heights on the elevations wherever the contour lines met the building. Then he had simply drawn the slope of the ground, or grade, by connecting his marks.

symbols   Even though the architect used notes to explain what everything meant, he also used symbols to indicate the materials that would be used. For example:

LIST OF ABBREVIATIONS

AFF   - ABOVE FINISH FLOOR
BOTT. - BOTTOM
CER.   - CERAMIC
C.H.   - COUNTER HEIGHT
CONC. - CONCRETE
C.T.   - CERAMIC TILE
DIA.   - DIAMETER
DN.   - DOWN
DWR - DRAWER
EL.   - ELEVATION
EXH.   - EXHAUST
EXT.GR.- EXTERIOR GRADE
FIN.FL.- FINISH FLOOR
FIN.GR.- FINISH GRADE
GAL.   - GALVANIZED
GR.   - GRILLE
H.C.   - HARD CORE
LAV.   - LAVATORY
MIN.   - MINIMUM
MT.   - MOUNTED
O.C.   - ON CENTER
OPP.   - OPERATED
P.H.   - PAPER HOLDER
PTD.PL.BD.- PAINTED PLASTER BOARD
Q.T.   - QUARRY TILE
RAD.   - RADIUS
RET.   - RETURN
R.O.   - ROUGH OPENING
T.B.   - TOWEL BAR
V.B.   - VAPOR BARRIER
VEN.   - VENEER
W.C.   - WATER CLOSET

LIST OF MATERIALS

CONCRETE

ROUGH LUMBER

FINISHED LUMBER

PLYWOOD

BRICK

CONCRETE BLOCK

FERROUS METAL

BATT INSULATION

These symbols were helpful because, by just glancing at the drawings, the builder would immediately see how it was constructed.

It was very important that everything be entirely clear, since the drawings were the guide the builder would follow to build the house. For this reason, the architect used notes to explain things wherever he couldn't describe something accurately with drawings.

scales   Because things could not be shown full size, the drawings had to be reduced to a small scale. The architect reduced some plans to one-hundredth of the actual building size, and marked them "scale" 1:100; where he wanted to show the same plan at a larger size, he reduced the actual building conditions to one-fiftieth, and marked these "scale" 1:50. In cases where even more detail was required, he showed the conditions at one-twentieth, or one-fifth or even at one-half the size of real life, indicating each, respectively as scale 1:20 or 1:5 or 1:2.

This page, without the binding, measures 215 millimeters by 279 millimeters. To illustrate the principle of "scale," the page would look like this, at different reductions:

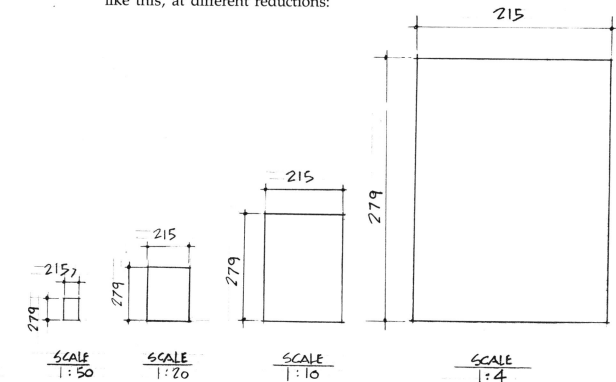

Since the drawings in this book had to be reduced to fit the page sizes, they are not shown at any standard scale. For this reason, a little graphic "scale" has been introduced near each drawing so that the reader can use it for measuring.

detail drawings

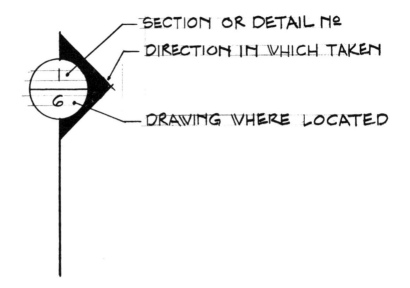

SECTION OR DETAIL Nº
DIRECTION IN WHICH TAKEN
DRAWING WHERE LOCATED

Details were usually sections drawn at a larger scale of part of the building. Sometimes they were cut to show how a place was constructed, and other times the section was taken to show the construction from an angle not seen elsewhere. For example, to see what happened at the side of a door, where the doorframe fit into the wall (called the jamb), there was a section through the jamb, looking down at it to show how it was constructed. When it was necessary to show how the top of the door (called the head) was fitted into the wall above it, a section was cut through the head, looking at the construction from the side.

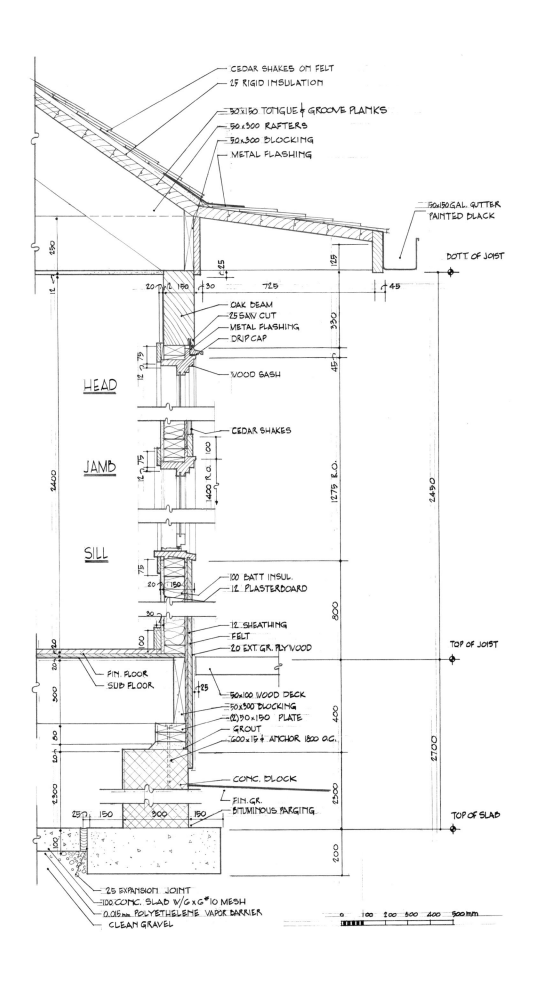

CEDAR SHAKES ON FELT
25 RIGID INSULATION
50x150 TONGUE & GROOVE PLANKS
50x300 RAFTERS
50x300 BLOCKING
METAL FLASHING

150x150 GAL. GUTTER
PAINTED BLACK

BOTT. OF JOIST

250
12
20
12
150
30
725
45
125

OAK BEAM
25 SAW CUT
METAL FLASHING
DRIP CAP
WOOD SASH

330
45

HEAD
12
75

JAMB
12
75
100

CEDAR SHAKES

1400 R.O.

1275 R.O.

2450

2400

SILL
75
20
150

100 BATT INSUL.
12 PLASTERBOARD

800

30
100

12 SHEATHING
FELT
20 EXT. GR. PLYWOOD

TOP OF JOIST

200
200

FIN. FLOOR
SUB FLOOR

500
25

50x100 WOOD DECK
50x300 BLOCKING
(2) 50x150 PLATE
GROUT
600x15 Ø ANCHOR 1800 O.C.

400

80
20

2700

2300

CONC. BLOCK

FIN. GR.
BITUMINOUS PARGING

2500

TOP OF SLAB

250
150
300
150

200

100

25 EXPANSION JOINT
100 CONC. SLAB W/6x6 #10 MESH
0.015mm POLYETHELENE VAPOR BARRIER
CLEAN GRAVEL

0   100   200   300   400   500 mm

electrical plan

The ELECTRICAL PLAN explained to the electrician the location of everything that required wiring. On the drawing, the dotted curves were an indication of which switch was supposed to turn on what light.

As a guide, the architect prepared an index, which was used to identify the various symbols he used on the plan.

Since some lights were fluorescent fixtures, others were recessed in the ceiling, and others were fancy chandeliers hanging from the ceiling, the architect listed his recommendations in the lighting schedule, so that the electrician could be sure to install the right light in the right place.

LIGHT FIXTURE SCHEDULE						
TYPE	QUANT.	MFR.	CATALOGUE NR	BULB	FINISH	REMARKS
A	9	JOHN DOE	1409	75 W R30 FLOOD	STD.	—
B	13	do	1400 -75	do	do	—
C	5	do	5000 - H1 - 16"	200 W IF	do	—
D	4	do	5000 - H1 - 14"	do	do	—
E	2	do	C - 5	100 W ; G40 WHITE	do	—
F	6	do	2100 VA - 347	50 W ; R20	BLACK	—
G	1	do	2100 VA - 448	75 W ; R30 FLOOD	do	—
H	2	do	PERF. METAL	100 W IF	WHITE	—
J	1	do	CF - 10	100 W IF	do	—
K	5	do	CS - 6	do	do	—
L	4	do	MC	75 W IF	do	—
M	8	—	—	50 W IF	—	PORC. SOCKET

ELECTRICAL SYMBOLS

- -�‑ LIGHT FIXTURE
- ⏦ UTILITY OUTLET
- ⏦CH COUNTER HEIGHT UTILITY OUTLET
- ⊙ FLOOR OUTLET
- ᛉ FLOODLIGHT
- ⌽ WALL SWITCH
- ⌽₃ TWO WAY WALL SWITCH
- ⌽₄ THREE WAY WALL SWITCH

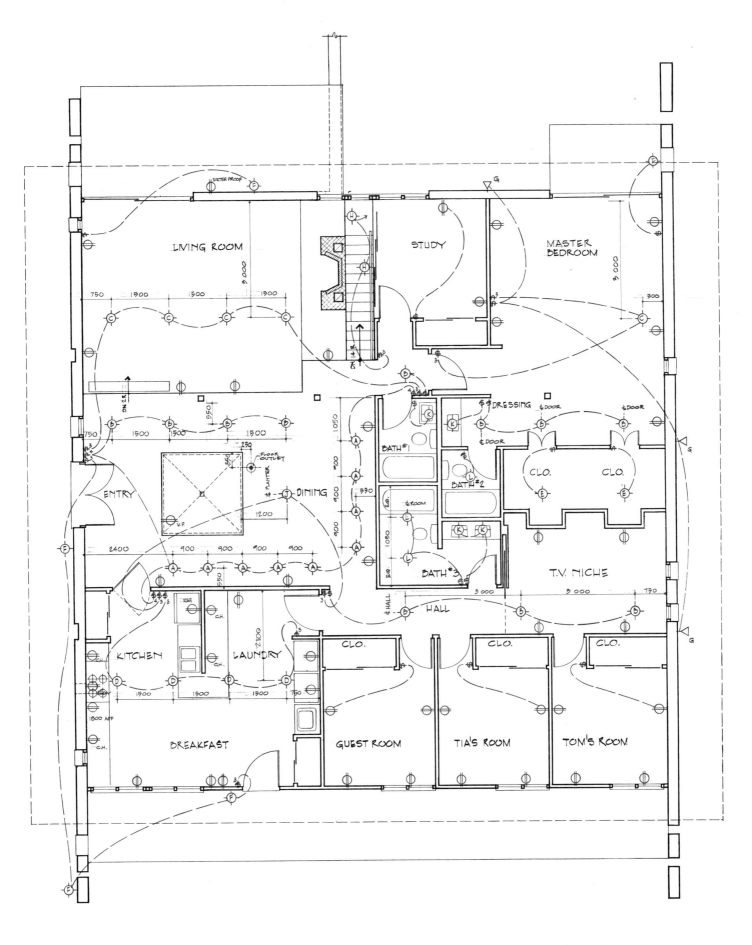

plumbing plan

The PLUMBING PLAN of the basement showed how the piping was arranged in the house. On this drawing, one could follow the pipe that brought the water from the street to the water meter, which recorded how much water was being used. From the meter, other pipes distributed the water to the different parts of the house. One pipe brought the water to the hot water heater, where it would be heated before it moved on to the various places where hot water was needed. The cold water, on the other hand, went directly to its destination from the meter.

A water meter was necessary only because Mr. Kummerfeld would be buying the water from the city or the water company. If there had been no water to buy, he would have had to dig a well on the property; and then no meter would have been needed to keep track of how much water was used.

The PLUMBING PLAN also described the pipe system used to remove the water from the bathrooms and kitchen. Since the street did not have a sewer, a septic tank would be used instead. This is a big concrete container, which is buried in the ground. The solid part of the waste settles on the bottom of the tank while the liquids flow on to another buried tank called a cesspool, or through some clay pipes, from which they seep into the ground and become part of Nature.

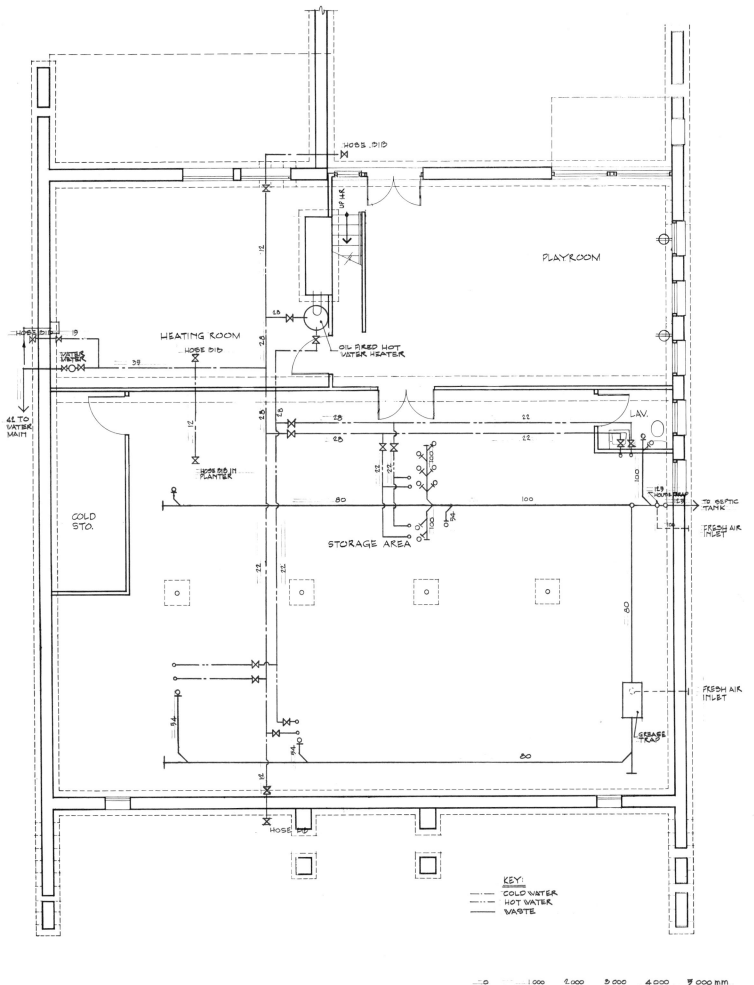

HOSE BIB

PLAYROOM

UP 14 R

HEATING ROOM

HOSE BIB

OIL FIRED HOT
WATER HEATER

HOSE BIB   15

WATER
METER

LAV.

HOUSE TRAP

35

TO SEPTIC
TANK

42 TO
WATER
MAIN

HOSE BIB IN
PLANTER

FRESH AIR
INLET

COLD
STO.

STORAGE AREA

FRESH AIR
INLET

GREASE
TRAP

HOSE BIB

KEY:
COLD WATER
HOT WATER
WASTE

0   1 000   2 000   3 000   4 000   5 000 mm

heating plan

The HEATING PLAN of the basement showed the furnace, which would suck in fresh outdoor air, heat it, and blow it through metal ducts to the registers in the rooms above. The ducts, which are shown in the basement HEATING PLAN, are rectangular tubes hung near the ceiling.

So that the warm air already in the house would not be wasted, part of it would be returned through return ducts to the furnace, where it would be mixed with fresh air, reheated, and reused in the house.

There are other ways of heating houses. Sometimes pipes are used to bring hot water or steam from the furnace to the radiators in the rooms, and sometimes each room has its own electric heater.

However, the architect recommended the hot-air system in the Kummerfelds' house because the ducts that would carry hot air in winter could also be used for cooled air in summer. By just adding a cooling unit to the system, the Kummerfelds could cool the house by simply turning off the furnace and switching on the air-conditioner.

The first floor HEATING PLAN showed openings in the floors that would be covered by metal grilles. These openings were the registers through which hot air would be blown up from the basement to warm the rooms.

The registers were usually under the windows, because that would be the area of the room that would be the coldest.

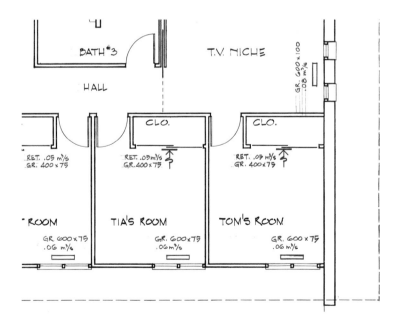

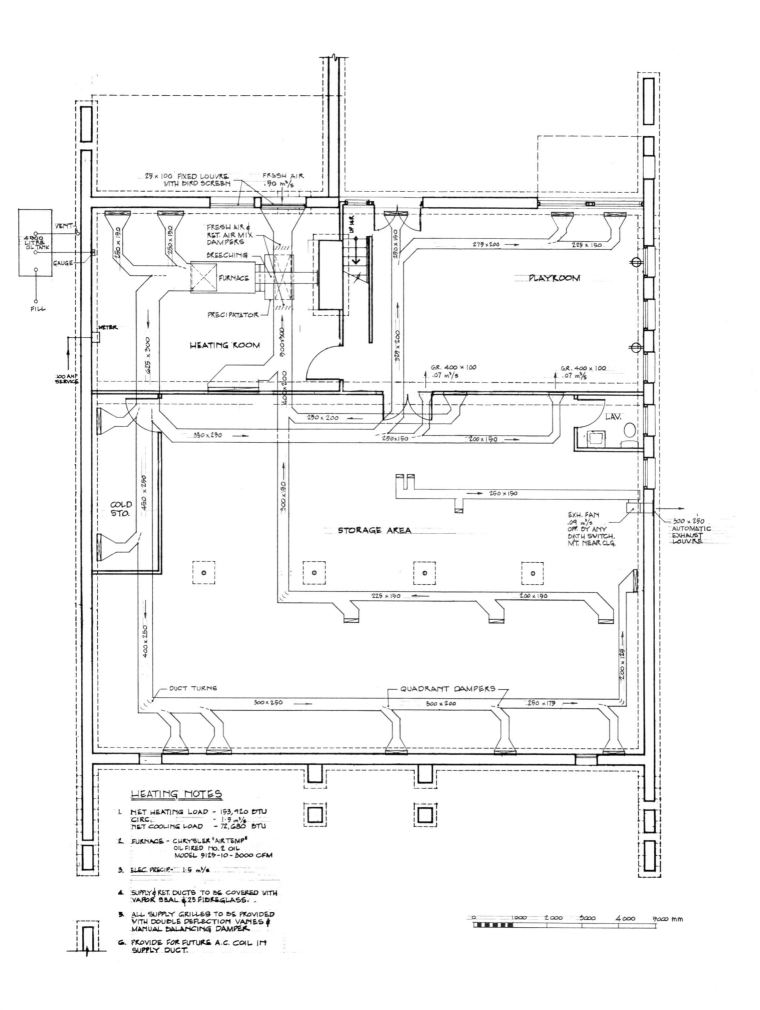

25 × 100 FIXED LOUVRE
WITH BIRD SCREEN

FRESH AIR
.50 m³/s

4500
LITRE
OIL TANK

VENT

GAUGE

FILL

METER

100 AMP
SERVICE

150 × 150

250 × 150

625 × 300

HEATING ROOM

FRESH AIR &
RET. AIR MIX
DAMPERS

BREECHING

FURNACE

PRECIPITATOR

UP 14 R.

150 × 150

320 × 200

279 × 200

225 × 150

PLAYROOM

GR. 400 × 100
.07 m³/s

GR. 400 × 100
.07 m³/s

LAV.

250 × 200

450 × 250

COLD
STO.

550 × 250

300 × 150

230 × 200

250 × 150

200 × 150

250 × 150

STORAGE AREA

EXH. FAN
.09 m³/s
OPP. BY ANY
BATH SWITCH.
MT. NEAR CLG.

300 × 250
AUTOMATIC
EXHAUST
LOUVRE

225 × 150

200 × 150

200 × 125

400 × 250

DUCT TURNS

QUADRANT DAMPERS

300 × 250

300 × 200

250 × 175

<u>HEATING NOTES</u>

1. NET HEATING LOAD - 153,920 BTU
   CIRC.   - 1.5 m³/s
   NET COOLING LOAD - 72,680 BTU

2. FURNACE - CHRYSLER "AIRTEMP"
   OIL FIRED No. 2 OIL
   MODEL 5125-10 - 3000 CFM

3. ELEC. PRECIP- 1.5 m³/s

4. SUPPLY & RET. DUCTS TO BE COVERED WITH
   VAPOR SEAL & 25 FIBREGLASS.

5. ALL SUPPLY GRILLES TO BE PROVIDED
   WITH DOUBLE DEFLECTION VANES &
   MANUAL BALANCING DAMPER

6. PROVIDE FOR FUTURE A.C. COIL IN
   SUPPLY DUCT.

1000   2000   3000   4000   5000 mm

doors

A door is a door. Or is it?

A front door differs from a kitchen door because it has special locks and handles on it and is often decorated with panels and little windows. It is also more solid than all the interior doors because it is specially designed to keep out the wind, the rain and burglars.

Bathroom doors can be locked from the inside only, bedroom doors from both sides, and closet doors sometimes have locks on the outside—and other times they have no locks at all. Most doors are on hinges and swing in, others swing out, while some others swing both in and out. Other doors don't swing at all but slide on tracks.

What door goes where? How could the builder tell?

The architect gave each door on the floor plan its own special number, and then prepared a door schedule where he described each door and its special features.

DOOR Nº	PANELS	SIZE	TYPE	CONST.	FINISH	BUCK	TH'LD.	HDW.	REMARKS
D-1	2	726 x 2040	PANELED	SOLID OAK	STAIN	WOOD	OAK	A	W'THSTP.
D-2	2	726 x 2040	GL. PANEL	PINE	PAINT	do	do	B	do
D-3	1	826 x 2040	DUTCH DOOR	do	do	do	do	C	W/GL. PANEL
D-4	1	826 x 2040	FLUSH/200 x 200 GL. PNL	S.C. OAK VEN.	STAIN	do	-	D	D'BL. ACTING
D-5	1	826 x 2040	FLUSH	H.C.	do	do	-	E	-
D-6	1	826 x 2040	do	do	do	do	-	do	-
D-7	1	726 x 2040	do	S.C.	PAINT	do	MARBLE	F	UNDERCUT 15
D-8	2	375 x 2040	LOUVRED	PINE	do	do	-	G	-
D-9	1	1200 x 2040	FLUSH	H.C. OAK. VEN.	STAIN	do	-	H	SLIDING
D-10	1	826 x 2040	do	H.C.	PAINT	do	OAK	E	-
D-11	2	726 x 2040	do	H.C. OAK. VEN.	STAIN	do	-	J	-
D-12	2	726 x 2040	do	do	do	do	-	K	SLIDING
D-13	2	826 x 2040	do	do	do	do	-	do	do
D-14	2	626 x 2040	do	do	do	do	-	do	do
D-15	2	2900 x 2400	SLIDING	ALUMINUM	ANODIZED	ALUM.	ALUM.	STD.	-
D-16	2	2900 x 2040	do	do	do	do	do	do	-

finish schedules

The architect also made a finish schedule on which he indicated how the surfaces in each space were to be finished. What floor would have carpeting, which wall would be painted, and which would be tiled or paneled. The schedule explained it all.

SPACE	FLOOR	BASE	WALLS	CEILING	REMARKS
ENTRY - DINING	Q.T.	100 WOOD	P'TD. PL. BD.	P'TD. PL. BD.	ALL WOOD BEAMS, POSTS ETC.-CLEAR STAIN
LIVING ROOM	OAK	do	do	STRUCTURE (SEALED)	SLATE HEARTH
STUDY	do	do	do	P'TD. PL. BD.	-
MASTER BEDROOM	do	do	do	STRUCTURE (SEALED)	-
DRESSING	do	do	do	P'TD. PL. BD.	-
ALL CLOSETS	do	do	do	do	Q.T. ON KITCHEN CLOS. FLOORS.
T.V. NICHE	do	do	do	do	-
HALL	Q.T./OAK	do	do	do	-
TOM'S ROOM	OAK	do	do	do	-
TIA'S ROOM	do	do	do	do	-
GUEST ROOM	do	do	do	do	-
KITCHEN-BK'FST ROOM	Q.T.	150 Q.T.	P'TD. PL. BD./C.T.	STRUCTURE	FOR TILE AREAS SEE KITCHEN ELEV.
BATH #1	C.T.	C.T.	do	P'TD. PL. BD.	-
BATH #2	do	do	do	do	-
BATH #3	do	do	do	do	-
HEATING ROOM	P'TD. CONC.	-	P'TD. PL. BD/BLK	P'TD. PL. BD.	-
PLAYROOM	V.A.T.	100 WOOD	P'TD. PL. BD.	do	-
LAV.	C.T.	C.T.	P'TD. PL. BD./C.T.	do	-
COLD STORAGE	P'TD. CONC.	-	P'TD. PL. BD/BLK	do	-
STORAGE AREA		do	-	do	-

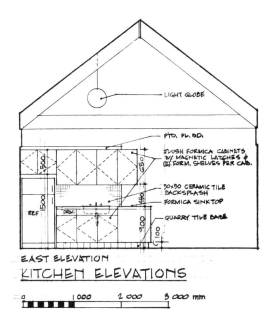

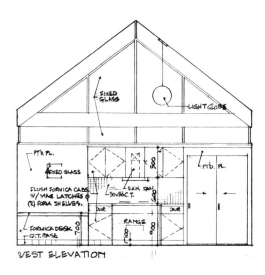

EAST ELEVATION
KITCHEN ELEVATIONS

0   1 000   2 000   3 000 mm

kitchens and bathrooms

Much effort and time can be spent selecting all the right water closets, the right sinks, the right color tiles, medicine cabinets, toilet paper holders and all the items that have to be installed in every bathroom in the house.

On the drawings, the architect showed exactly where he wanted everything located.

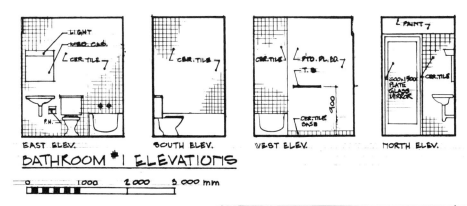

EAST ELEV.   SOUTH ELEV.   WEST ELEV.   NORTH ELEV.

BATHROOM #1 ELEVATIONS

0   1000   2 000   3 000 mm

PLUMBING FIXTURE SCHEDULE		
FIXTURE	TYPE	TRIM
BATH	CRANE 2-78	8-1300 (CRITERION)
W.C.	CRANE 3-112	SEAT 3-887
LAV.	CRANE 1-272-D	8-1020-A (CRITERION)

All of the drawings, specifications and schedules had been prepared by the architect and his draftsmen. On simple jobs, such as the design of the Kummerfeld residence, the architect and his draftsmen usually have enough knowledge to be able to handle all aspects of the work. They can calculate the size of the pipes, the strength of the beams, and select the type of planting and lighting that is best for the house.

engineers and designers

However, on larger and more complex structures the architect usually consults with specialists from different areas. For the calculations of the structure, he calls on structural engineers for help. For the heating and air conditioning, he will ask the advice of a mechanical engineer, and he may even require the services of a specialist engineer to work with him on the plumbing and electrical problems.

There are landscape architects who work with architects on the design of the exterior settings of buildings. Landscape architects know about drainage of the land, about what plants will grow well with little sunlight and which flowers will provide the right color all summer long.

For the inside of the building, there are interior designers who work on the selection and arrangement of colors, lighting and furnishings. They work closely with both the architect and the client; and together they can give the right finishing touches to a new building.

specifications   Who will pay for the cleaning of the windows when the building is finished? Who is responsible for the insurance in case the house burns down during construction? How many coats of what type of paint will be used in the different areas? How much cement is needed for the concrete mix? Are the pipes made of copper or plastic? What quality of window does the builder have to install? Who has to go to the city building department to get the permit to build?

Since the answers to these and many other questions cannot be shown on the drawings either graphically or by notes, the architect also prepares a written text that gives a full explanation. This document is called the specifications.

To help him prepare this material, the architect keeps reference books, manufacturers' catalogs and a sample collection in his office. He also frequently consults with representatives of manufacturers who make the many things that go into a building; they explain to him the latest developments in the field of building technology.

Chapter Three

"Wow," said Mr. Kummerfeld, when the family had gone over the completed work. "I didn't realize how much goes into the making of a house."

"I'm glad you do now," replied the architect. And he added, only half-joking, "Maybe you'll feel less like complaining about my fee."

Dad smiled and nodded. Then he said seriously, "I hope I can afford all this. Somehow all these plans make this look like an expensive house."

"I think it can be built for the figure you felt you could pay," the architect said. "It ought to fit your budget. We'll soon know. I think we should get in touch with at least three good reliable builders and ask them for bids. Bids, he went on to explain to Tia and Tom, "are the prices that the builders would charge to build the building as described on the drawings and specifications."

budget

Mr. Kummerfeld nodded. "Yes, I agree."

"How long will that take?" asked Tia, exasperated. Weren't they ever going to get around to making the house? Were they forever going to be talking, drawing, and never doing anything about it?

Tom just frowned.

"Be patient just a little longer," said the architect.

So three builders chosen by the Kummerfelds and the architect were asked for bids. The one who promised to build the house, just as it was laid out in the plans for the lowest price, would be the one asked to build the house. Each builder was given a complete set of plans and specifications to use for making his cost estimate. And after three weeks of studying material, each of them arrived at a price for which he could build the house including his profit for doing the work.

"But even the lowest one is over our budget," said Mom. "What are we going to do now?" She sounded as impatient as Tia and Tom had been for a long time.

"Let's talk to the builder with the lowest bid," the architect proposed. "Maybe there's something we can do about it."

And there was. After a lot of talk, the builder suggested that they **choosing a contractor** leave out the air conditioning for the present. It could always be put in later. It seemed like a good solution. With daisies and an apple tree and an inside garden, who needed air conditioning.

There was another contract to sign, this time with the builder. And then the house could really be started.

"Do you have enough money now?" asked Tia, when her father came home from signing the papers.

"Well, I don't," said Mr. Kummerfeld. "But the bank does. No one has enough money to build a house —or at least most people don't. I don't earn as much in four or five years put together as this house will cost. And we have to have money for eating and clothes, too. But the bank will give us most of the money we need. It's called a mortgage. And I'll pay it back to them, giving them some extra money called interest, in return for their letting me have the money when I need it. In twenty-five years, if all goes well, the mortgage will be paid up. In the meantime, if I don't pay for some reason, the bank will have the house for security and they can take the house and sell it to get their money back."

Tia looked alarmed. "But I thought it was going to be our house, not **a mortgagor** the bank's house."

"It will be our house. As long as we pay them, regularly, part of the money we owe or don't sell the house to someone else."

Tia still looked upset.

"Don't worry. I expect to be able to pay. And so does the bank. Or the people there wouldn't have given me the money in the first place."

It was winter when the building of the house really began. The whole family drove out a couple of days after the builders had started. There were stakes driven into the ground to mark the outside of the house. And a big bulldozer was digging up the ground. Tia's daisy patch was a mess.

"The daisies will never come up again," moaned Tia.

"Oh yes they will," said the builder, who just happened to be there. "We'll put everything back together again just the way it was."

Tom was not so worried because the builder had put a little fence around his apple tree to protect it.

"Will you be here all the time to watch and supervise?" Tom asked.

"No, that won't be necessary," the builder answered. "I'll keep my eye on it, of course. I don't want anything to go wrong. But my main job is to find other people to do the work and make sure they do it right. I'm **subcontractors** what's called the general contractor. I find subcontractors who each do their own special things, and my job is to coordinate their work. Right now we have an excavator working. Then we'll have the masons in. And so on."

The family visited often, and at last the house really did seem to be growing. First came the masons who poured the concrete for footings on which the walls would rest, and who made the basement. The carpenters followed and built the wooden floor of the house and the framing, with studs, which are the wood uprights for the walls. When they were in place, the Kummerfelds could see where the walls would be and where the openings for the doors and windows were. Once the walls were up, the men hurried to put on a roof, to protect the house from the snow, which was beginning to fall on the meadow.

Sometimes when the family came, they found the architect there, because he, like the general contractor, wanted to be sure that everything was being done according to his plans.

As the work went on, the electricians put in the wiring and the switches, the plumbers connected the piping and the bathroom fixtures, the sheet metal men put in the ducts for the heating. It was confusing, messy, and hard to find your way around in until the walls were smoothly finished with tape and spackle. The carpenters then installed the doorframes and hung the doors and windows; the cabinetmaker brought the kitchen cabinets, which he had built in his shop to fit the space for them. And then everything was ready for the painters. Once the painters were done, the Kummerfelds could move in.

The Kummerfelds didn't visit the house while it was being painted. They were too busy packing to move. They didn't even get there to see the builder bring in his bulldozer again to restore the meadow to its original shape. And the whole family was surprised when they drove out the night before they were to move in, to see the house looking so finished. The concrete men had even laid the driveway and the walks. They weren't hard enough, so no one could walk on them. But by morning they would be ready.

moving in   It was spring then, when the house was ready and the Kummerfelds moved in. It had taken almost a year from the day they had first seen the lot to the day they could put their furniture on the moving van and feel that they had a house that was going to be right for them.

The morning they moved in, they got there before the moving van arrived. The house looked as if it had been resting comfortably in the meadow almost forever. It seemed to belong. It was beautiful.

When they went inside they thought again that it was just as they had imagined it would be. It felt just right.

Dad, with his arm around Mom's shoulders, walked to the living room, which was on the exact spot where they had stood a year before. They stopped and admired the view into the valley that stretched out beyond.

"What a place for a living room!" said Mom.

"Why not ours?" said Dad.

Tom was the only one who didn't come in. He was in the tree already planning construction of another house—the tree house.

And when Tia ran to her room, which was just on the spot she had picked out for it, there outside the window were a few daisies. Not all the daisies that had been there the year before, because a lot had happened to the meadow in the meantime. But there were enough to tell her that someday there would be as many again as she had once seen. And now they were her daisies, to look out on every day, from a room that had all the space she needed for everything.

Glossary

Batt Insulation Loose material such as glass wool or fibers used as insulation, contained in long flexible paper or foil "bags" that fit between rafters, joists or studs. *See* insulation.

Beam A major horizontal structural member, on which joists or other minor structural members rest. *See* structural system.

Bearing Synonym for supporting

Binder A temporary agreement subject to a permanent contract

Bituminous Any of a number of materials made from tars or asphalts used for waterproofing

Block A basis building unit concrete used to construct walls. Most blocks are larger than bricks and are usually hollow to make them easier to lift.

Blocking Usually short pieces of wood used to hold something in proper position, as opposed to long pieces such as "plates," which offer continuous support

cm *See* centimeter

Centimeter One-hundredth of a meter or 100 centimeters (cm) = 1 meter (m); (2.54 centimeters = 1 inch)

Closing The meeting at which an agreement is finalized and a contract is signed

Column A vertical (upright) structural member of wood, steel or concrete. *See* structural system.

Commission The fee paid to someone authorized to sell real estate for its owner

Concrete A mixture of cement, sand, gravel and water that hardens into stonelike material. Steel mesh or rods are used in concrete for reinforcement.

Contract A written agreement between two or more parties that becomes legally binding

Deed A contract that transfers real estate from one owner to another

Elevation
  meaning 1 A view of the building, looking directly at it. A direct projection from the floor plan showing the exact relationship without distortion

Elevation
  meaning 2 The height of any part of the building or land in relationship to a fixed point

Exhaust Fan   A fan in the wall or ceiling that draws out, or exhausts used air from bathrooms or kitchens

Expansion Joint   A space filled with a flexible material used at the edge between the concrete wall and the floor, designed to allow the slab to expand and contract as the temperature changes; otherwise, without the room to move, the concrete would crack

Fascia   A horizontal band at the edge of a roof used for either decorative purposes or for protection of vulnerable parts of the building from the weather

Felt   A heavy paperlike material impregnated with bituminous compounds, used to waterproof roofs, exterior walls and basement slabs. "Built-up" roofs are created by building up several layers, or "plies" of felt by bonding them into one continuous surface with asphalt or tar.

Fixed Glass   A panel of glass used like a window, except that it cannot be opened or closed

Flashing   Sheet metal or other durable material used to prevent water from getting through joints where the two exterior surfaces meet, such as the intersection of the roof and the chimney

Footing   A concrete base used under foundation walls and columns to distribute the load to the supporting ground. *See* structural system.

Foundation Wall   A heavy wall of masonry or concrete, designed to be strong enough to carry the load from above and frequently to resist the soil pressure from one side

Insulation   Any of many materials, included in the wall, floor or ceiling construction with the property to reduce the movement of heat, cold or sound from one place to another

Joist   One of a series of evenly spaced horizontal structural members that support the floors and flat ceilings. *See* structural system.

Lally Column   A square or round steel tube filled with concrete for extra strength, used as a structural column

Lintel   A horizontal structural member similar to a beam, specifically used to carry the load over wide openings in walls

Lot   A parcel of land, sometimes part of a larger subdivision of property

Louver   An opening with slanted slats, which allow air to pass through freely while preventing rain from entering. Louvers are also used to permit air circulation into spaces that require visual privacy.

m   *See* meter

mm   *See* millimeter

millimeter   One-thousandth of a meter or 10 millimeters (mm) = 1 centimeter (cm); (25.4 millimeters = 1 inch)

Masonry   Anything built of brick, stone or block

Mesh A net of steel wires used to reinforce concrete slabs

Meter 1 meter (m) = 100 centimeters (cm) or 1000 millimeters (1 meter = 39.37 inches)

o.c. A frequently used abbreviation meaning "on center," indicating distance from the center line of one thing to the center line of the next

Outlet The terminal point of the electrical wiring on a finished surface into which electrical fixtures or appliances can be plugged

Parging A heavy coat of cement or bituminous material spread on masonry for protection and waterproofing

Partition Any non-bearing interior wall or room divider

Perimeter Insulation A continuous strip of rigid insulation used all around the building at the basement walls to prevent loss of heat. *See* insulation.

Pier A short masonry column

Pitch The slope or angle

Plaster Board Or "sheetrock" is a ridgid panel made of gypsum, fibers and paper nailed to the studs, or joists, used for the joint between two panels. It is covered with paper and smoothed over with a paste called "spackle." When painted, the panels of plaster board will appear as one clean unbroken surface.

Plate Refers to a piece of lumber laid flat on top of a wall to distribute the weight it receives from loads above

Plywood A sheet material or panel built up of three or more thin layers of wood glued together with grains going in alternate directions for additional strength. Exterior grade plywood is made with waterproof glue.

Polyethelene A plastic used in thin but strong sheets for moistureproofing floors and walls

Post A wood column

Rafters Sloping joists that support the roof. *See* structural system.

Roofing Generally refers to any material that covers the roof

Real Estate Land, complete with any building that may be on it

Sash The movable part of a window

Saw cut An indentation on the bottom of a beam that causes the water to drip off, preventing it from dribbling back to the building

Sheathing A material, such as planking or plywood, that is fastened to the studs of a wall or the rafters of a roof, which stiffens the structure while providing a base for attachment for the finished covering material

"Sheetrock" *See* Plaster Board

Shingle A rectangular thin wood or other material that is used to cover the exterior walls and roofs. The upper shingle always laps part of the one below.

Skylight   A window in the roof

Slab   A continuously flat area of concrete

Structural   A term, which applies to every part of a building that participates in making it stand up. Structural members rarely work alone, and are usually part of a structural system.

Structural System   The teamwork by different structural elements required to hold the building in place and support its own weight and the superimposed loads. It is a term that applies to every type of construction, whether the structure is of concrete, wood or steel. There are infinite variations of how the various elements work together, but a description of a typical wood house can be used to explain the principle.

Every roof must be designed to carry a load, such as snow.

The roof load is transferred through the finished roofing material to a relatively thin layer of planks or plywood called roof sheathing.

The sheathing is supported at frequent intervals to keep it from bending by rafters or roof joists. The difference between rafters and roof joists is that the parts are called rafters where they are sloped, and joists where the roof is flat.

The rafters or roof joists are supported either by a bearing wall, which is designed to be strong enough to take the weight down, or beams, which are horizontal members strong enough to carry the collective load of many joists. Frequently, the beams rest on bearing walls, but mostly they are supported by columns.

The columns are vertical supports of wood or steel that carry the load from one or more beams straight down. On the way down, they may pick up loads from one or more floors. At the bottom, each column rests on its own footing.

The footings under the columns are thick concrete bases that distribute their load over a large area of soil. The greater the load and the softer the soil, the bigger the area over which the load will have to be spread.

On the way down, the bearing walls may also collect additional loads from one or more floors; when they reach the level of the basement ceiling, the bearing walls rest on foundations.

The foundations are masonry or concrete walls, strong enough not only to support the load from above, but also to resist the pressure from the ground outside the building. The foundations also rest on footings, which in turn are wider than the walls so that they can spread the load over a greater area of soil.

Going back upstairs to a typical floor; the floor load, which is greater than a roof load, is transferred through the finished flooring to a subfloor of plywood or planking, which is supported by floor joists that are stronger than roof joists because they carry a bigger load. They serve the same function and transfer their load via the beams or bearing walls, the columns and foundations to the footings.

Using his understanding of the principles as a tool, the architect can make up variations of the basic systems to get special effects. In the Kummerfeld house, for example, there are no rafters because the ceiling planks were designed to be strong enough to carry the roof load directly to beams, which then blend into a more or less standard system. By doing this, the architect was able to get a high ceiling, where the structural members are visible and contribute to the experience of an exciting space.

Stucco A mixture of cement, lime, sand and water that hardens to become both a waterproof and decorative finish material

Studs Evenly spaced upright supports that form the skeleton for walls and partitions

T & G *See* "Tongue and Groove"

Ties Structural members used to "tie" others into place. In this house they keep the roof beams from spreading.

Title A document that indicates the right of ownership of real estate

Tongue and Groove Abbreviated as T & G, refers to the relationship of the shaped edges to two adjacent planks, where the "tongue" of one fits into a groove in the other, the result being a plane without any through joints, even when the planks shrink. (Note that all wood shrinks as it dries out, or expands in humid weather when it absorbs moisture.)

Vapor Barrier A thin sheet of plastic or layer of felt that is used to prevent moisture penetration

Vent A pipe or duct that leads undesirable gases or air to the exterior

Zoning A legal restriction imposed on certain areas of land limiting the nature of its use